The Steward's Seat

12 Anchors for Bridging Faith & Leadership

Devotional Journal

Ashely D. Teasdel

I0531277

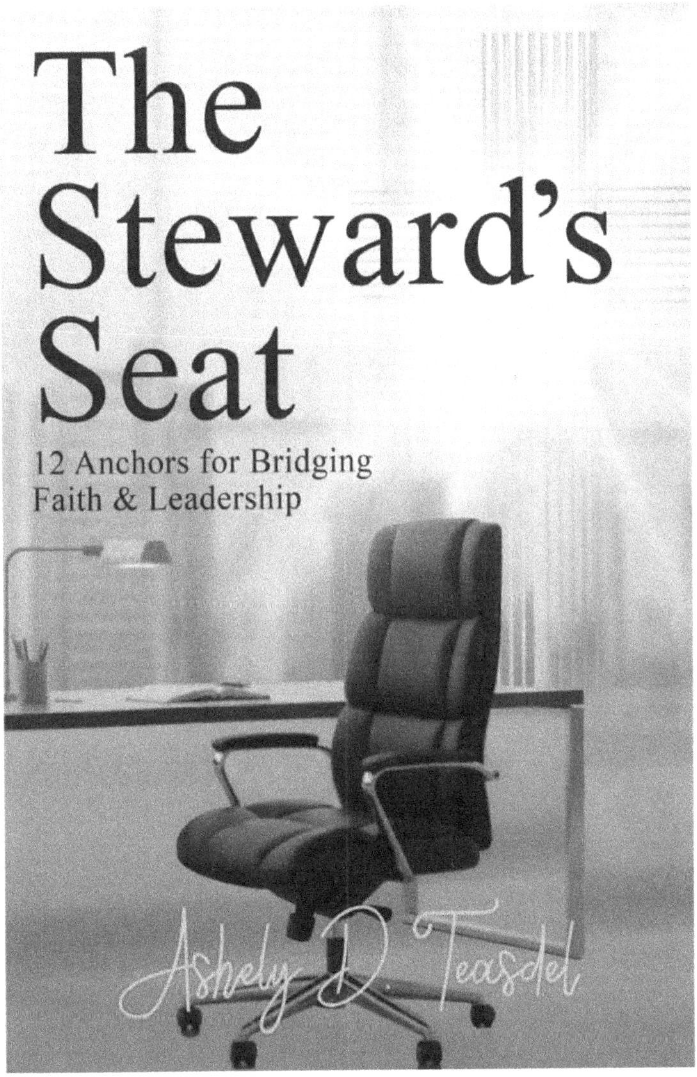

The
Steward's
Seat

12 Anchors for Bridging
Faith & Leadership

Ashely D. Teasdel

The Steward's Seat

Dedication

To my family, the foundation beneath every step of this journey.

To my husband, John. Your unwavering support, steadfast belief in me, and constant encouragement have been a source of strength and joy. Thank you for standing with me, championing my calling, and loving me so well.

To my daughters, Janelle and Aubrey. You inspire me every day. I see the leaders you are becoming, full of thoughtfulness, faith, wisdom, and grace. I pray that you always walk with purpose, courage, and a heart turned toward God.

To my father, who has been both natural and spiritual covering. Your prayers, guidance, and example of steadfast faith have shaped the path I walk.

To my mother, my closest confidant and friend. Thank you for your wisdom, your presence, and your ability to speak truth with love.

To the executive mentors, teachers, friends, and guides who have poured into me across seasons. Your influence is woven into the pages of my life and, in many ways, into the pages of this devotional journal. I am grateful for every lesson, every conversation, and every moment you believed in the leader I could become.

This work is a testament to what God forms in us through the people He places around us.

The Steward's Seat

A Letter to the Reader & Leader

This devotional journal is written for you: the **steward-leader** who faithfully serves in roles that carry immense responsibility but may not always carry the spotlight. You are the integrators, the implementers, and the steady voice of reason in rooms filled with passion. You uniquely interpret vision and bridge it to execution. You're committed to building systems that are strong, reliable, and sustainable, along with relationships that are anchored in trust.

You're the steady presence others instinctively gravitate to — the one who brings alignment, focus, and calm when the moment feels uncertain. Your name may not always be front and center, but your fingerprints and footprints are everywhere. You lead through **presence and from commitment, not position.** That is no small calling; that is a sacred gift.

In Scripture, a steward is someone entrusted with the management and care of something valuable that does not fully belong to them. It is a role defined not by **control**, but by **trust**. Today, you occupy a similar space, responsible for guiding teams, managing complex decisions, nurturing culture, and protecting the integrity of a mission you have been called to carry.

Whether you are a chief of staff, a COO, an executive assistant, an assistant pastor, a chief administrator, a ministry leader, or a quiet leader within a fast-moving organization, this devotional is for you. It was created to acknowledge the sacred space you hold and the weight that comes with it. The work you do matters deeply. And more importantly, so does how you carry it.

This book is organized around **12 Anchors**: a practical and spiritual framework for your leadership. The number twelve is intentional. In the Bible, it represents divine order, governmental structure, and completeness. These anchors are designed to ground you, steady you, and remind you that your leadership has both *purpose* and *spiritual alignment*.

These are not just topics. They are truths I live by and ones I am still striving to perfect. A personal framework born from experience, faith, and the tension of learning in real time. Each anchor offers a moment to pause, reflect, and reconnect with the deeper meaning behind what you do, and who you are while doing it.

You may lead from the second chair, but your impact is first in line.

As a final resource, you will find a bonus chapter, *The Steward's Daily Armor*, which provides a blueprint for applying these twelve truths to your daily preparation.

Each anchor is intentionally structured to offer you a holistic moment of reflection and recalibration:

1. **Leadership Reflection + Biblical Connection:** Weaving together biblical narrative and modern leadership realities.
2. **Leadership in Real Life:** A practical section that translates spiritual insights into concrete, actionable practices for daily leadership. It explores how a core anchor takes shape in everyday action, demonstrating that the profound influence of leadership carries both great reward and weighty responsibility. It also guides you toward "leading whole," a sustainable approach that integrates your authentic self and values into every dimension of your life and work.
3. **A Closing Prayer:** An invitation into spiritual dialogue about what you're processing.
4. **Leadership Check-In:** A dedicated section of open-ended questions to assess your current posture, decisions, and challenges.
5. **Open Journal Space:** Room to process, document growth, and release what's been sitting on your heart.

This was uniquely woven together to offer both natural and spiritual support, clarity, flexible accountability, and a deeply personal leadership companion you can return to again and again. This isn't about proving yourself; it's about anchoring your soul for the journey. It is about finding clarity in the calling to lead without needing to validate your value.

In truth, there are few resources out there that speak directly to the sacred intersection where faith and leadership meet. Not just on Sundays or in special religious retreats, but in the daily decisions and responsibilities leaders carry. This devotion was created to be more than just inspiration. Let it be a companion, a guide, and a tool of spiritual encouragement and recalibration. May it give voice to what you carry, direction to how you lead, and strength to the parts of your soul that pour out the most.

I wrote this for every faithful leader who helps carry the responsibility, bridge gaps, and build legacies from the middle.

May you be reminded that God sees how you lead, and He honors it.

With sincere gratitude,

Ashely

Table of Contents

Every assignment faces moments of vulnerability. Stewards are called to protect, preserve, and uphold the foundational integrity that others may not fully see.

8. Boundaries and Renewal

Renewal is the discipline of governing your own capacity and building necessary boundaries to ensure you lead from fullness, not fatigue.

9. Loyalty with Integrity

Faithfulness is not blind silence. It is the courage to honor your assignment while remaining uncompromisingly true to the highest ethical standard.

10. Waiting – Trusting - Leading

Delays are not denials. Strategic patience forms leaders while waiting, revealing the necessary strategic timing.

11. Finishing Well

Leadership is measured not only by what we build but by how we release. Stewards conclude assignments with intentional wisdom and empowering grace.

12. Legacy from the Second Chair

True legacy is not about platform or power. It is about the enduring health of the system you built and the fidelity of your character.

13. BONUS Chapter – Daily Preparation:

The Stewards' Daily Armor: The Whole Armor of God

Anchor # 1

Entrusted to Lead

The Steward's Seat

Anchor 1: Entrusted to Lead: The Sacred Call of the Steward's Seat

Leadership Reflection + Biblical Connection

Leadership is often glamorized as the place where decisions are made, and accolades are won. But there is a kind of leadership that runs deeper. One that is steady, responsible, and grounded in trust. This is what I call the **Steward's Seat**: a role that isn't second class but carries its own type of authority. It is where vision becomes tangible, where expectation meets execution, and where leaders are called to manage faithfully. Over the course of my leadership journey, I've learned that this seat demands not only skill but integrity, consistency, discernment, and wisdom.

There is a magnitude that rests on the shoulders of those who serve in entrusted roles. I often describe it as the "*Steward's Seat*" because it is the place where influence and accountability meet. It's also where you don't just help carry the vision, you shape how it takes form day by day. You may not be the face of the mission, but you are the force that gives it structure, motion, and meaning. It isn't about chasing titles or proximity to power. It's about answering the call to stand in the middle, to translate direction into action, and to hold the line between vision and execution with grace and conviction.

When I think about what that kind of leadership looks like in its purest form, my mind always turns to Joseph. His journey began with promise and favor, yet it quickly turned toward hardship. He was gifted, even anointed, but his early confidence and commitment stirred jealousy in others. Betrayed by his brothers and sold into slavery, Joseph's life became a quick study in endurance. Still, at every stage, trust seemed to find him. In Potiphar's house, he was placed in charge of everything his master owned, and even when a false accusation led to his imprisonment, that same favor followed him. Genesis 39:20–23 tells us that while still a prisoner, Joseph was placed in charge of the very prison that confined him. The warden entrusted everything to his care, and whatever Joseph did, the Lord made it prosper.

That consistent thread of character while doing ordinary work with extraordinary faithfulness became the bridge to his next season. The same integrity that marked his service in prison caught the attention of Pharaoh when the moment of interpretation came. Joseph rose to become second-in-command over Egypt, not by ambition but by readiness. He interpreted Pharaoh's dreams with clarity, developed a plan for the years of abundance and famine, and administered the nation's resources with precision. Because of that stewardship, Egypt not only survived a global famine but became a refuge for others. His leadership preserved lives, strengthened a nation's stability, and extended influence far beyond Egypt's borders. What once looked like misfortune had been preparation for management at a higher level. That is the true mark of stewardship: leading faithfully wherever you are placed, until the fruit of that faithfulness blesses more than just you.

Joseph's story reminds me that leadership is rarely a straight line. Entrustment often begins in unexpected places, like in projects that feel too small to matter, in roles that stretch you, and in seasons that test your will and patience. Stewardship often grows in the background. It develops when you're asked to see vision through to the end. What God entrusted to Joseph in prison was the same faithfulness that would later sustain a kingdom. The setting changed, but the spirit of stewardship never did.

I've come to see and admire that the steward's seat can exist anywhere. It could be in an office, a classroom, or a conversation that calls for steady leadership. The call to be entrusted isn't about being first, it's about being faithful. It's leading with confidence anchored in purpose and humility anchored in trust. The leaders who truly transform cultures and communities aren't always the loudest or most visible. They are the ones who bring steadiness, wisdom, and care to everything placed in their hands. At its highest expression, leadership is stewardship; the daily, intentional honoring of what has been placed in your care.

Leadership in Real Life

How the Call Takes Shape in Everyday Leadership

Entrusted leadership doesn't announce itself; it reveals its strength in what it naturally sustains. It lives in the work no one else pauses to notice, in the details held together by someone who understands that responsibility is not glamorous but necessary. I often think of it as the quarterback of an organization, calling plays from the pocket, reading the field, adjusting when the moment shifts. It feels like the hand on the rudder, ensuring the organizational flow stays steady and true to the destination. You may not always see the subtle adjustments, but you can sense their influence in how everything moves together.

That is what stewardship looks like in real life. It is the leader who steadies a team, the assistant who manages momentum behind the scenes, or the chief administrator who makes sure big ideas don't lose their footing on the way to execution. I think sometimes this can frustrate others or be misunderstood as resistance, as if the steward is slowing progress or hesitating to advance the ball. But true stewardship has never been about slowing things down; it's about protecting what must endure. What I've learned is that a steward's strength isn't in *holding things back*, but in *holding everything together*. Their role is to safeguard purpose in motion, to keep the pace sustainable, the mission clear, and the foundation strong.

The Reward and the Responsibility

When you lead this way, trust begins to form around you almost without effort. People start to breathe easier because they know you are thinking ahead. They sense stability even when things feel uncertain. There is something fulfilling about watching a team or an organization find its rhythm because of the structure you quietly provided. When you serve well in the middle, you become the bridge between vision and execution. You learn over time and through various experiences how to bring calm and rhythm to movement.

Yet that same steadiness can carry a hidden cost. When you are the one who holds the line, people can forget that you have limits too. It can feel like you are carrying everyone else's load while trying to keep your own footing. I have lived that tension, where loyalty to the mission starts to overshadow care for myself. You begin to confuse faithfulness with fatigue, thinking they are the same thing. Over time, the joy that once energized you can start to fade in the background. It is hard to admit when the work you love begins to drain you, especially when others depend on your strength to stay standing.

Leading Whole

Healthy stewardship begins when you learn to lead from fullness instead of depletion. Renewal doesn't mean stepping away from purpose; it just means making space to hear clearly again. The best leaders I know have learned to treat restoration as a discipline, not a luxury. I've had to learn more quickly in the past few years than ever that stillness does not mean you are falling behind. It means you are allowing space for clarity to speak before the next move. Creating pauses for prayer, reflection, or quiet thought helps you realign what belongs on your plate and what can be shared. Stewardship at its best is shared stewardship; a team effort that honors both calling and capacity. When you lead from a rested spirit, you lead with discernment instead of reaction.

Joseph's story continues to remind me that this enduring faithfulness is only possible through continuous internal stewardship. The Bible consistently emphasizes: "*The Lord was with Joseph*." This divine presence, maintained through connection and unwavering reliance on God, is what allowed him to endure years of injustice without bitterness or self-corruption. His capacity for continuous excellence and internal stability (rejecting temptation and operating without ambition) is the truest form of self-stewardship. This enduring integrity is proof that his inner life was whole. I have learned through seasons of my own that rest is not a reward for finishing the work, but rather it is part of the work itself. When we lead from a place of wholeness, we find freedom to pause without guilt, to pray before we plan, and to believe that excellence and ease can coexist. God never asked us to prove our worth by how much we can handle. He simply asks us to honor Him by how well we handle what He has placed in our hands.

Prayer

Father,

Thank You for trusting me with the privilege of leadership. Thank You for the people, the projects, and the purpose You have placed within my reach. Some days the seat feels light. Other days it feels heavy, shaped by responsibility I did not ask for but know I must carry. In both, teach me to be faithful.

When I am tempted to rush, help me to slow down. When I feel unseen, remind me that You see. When I grow weary from managing what's mine and what sometimes feels belongs to another, remind me that it all belongs to You. Grant me wisdom to lead with discernment, courage to lead with integrity, and humility to lead with care.

May my stewardship reflect Your character. Let every decision I make honor the trust that has been given. Strengthen my hands to build what lasts and soften my heart to listen before I act.

Keep me grounded in Your presence, steady in purpose, and faithful in every season, from the unseen work to the visible outcomes. May I lead well where I am, knowing that the true measure of leadership is not the size of my influence but the posture of my heart. Amen.

Leadership Check-In

Take a moment to reflect on where your leadership is being stretched, tested, or refined. Use the prompts below to journal your thoughts and revisit your posture as a steward.

Reflection:

- What decision or responsibility am I currently carrying that doesn't fully belong to me, but still depends on me?
- How have I been showing up? Am I rushing to fix, or pausing to listen?
- Did I miss anything that needs revisiting with more care?
- Where might God be inviting me to lead with rest instead of resistance?
- What does faithfulness look like right now in this season, with what I have?

_____

_____

_____

_____

_____

The Steward's Seat

The Steward's Seat

Anchor 2: Called to Carry: The Steady Assignment of Vision-Aligned Leadership

Leadership Reflection + Biblical Connection

There is a particular kind of leadership that is designed to hold things together. Its power isn't rooted in visibility but in capacity; capacity to lift, steady, and advance what matters. This is the kind of leadership that embraces responsibility.

Many of us live here. We are the ones who interpret purpose and translate it into something real. We plan what others imagine, organize what others declare, and apply hard-won experiences to assess potential pitfalls, ensuring the mission is not only ambitious but built to last. And through it all, we lead without needing to possess. The work matters more than the credit. The mission matters more than the moment. It's not always easy, but it is significant.

While the world may use terms like "integrator," I believe this kind of leader is better described as a vision Carrier, someone entrusted with making purpose sustainable. The Carrier is rarely the originator or the final voice, but the one who strengthens, supports, refines, and guards what has been initiated. If the visionary plants the seed, the Carrier makes sure it can grow.

Priscilla, alongside her husband Aquila, offers us a powerful example of this kind of stewardship. We primarily know them as the trusted partners of the Apostle Paul, providing the essential infrastructure for his mission. Their home became Paul's base of operations, their tentmaking trade provided the shared funding, and they became the stable, reliable presence that allowed the mission to flourish wherever Paul traveled. Paul himself referred to them as his *"fellow workers in Christ Jesus,"* even commending them for risking their lives for him (Romans 16:3–4).

In Acts 18, we see their Carrier role in action when they encounter Apollos, an eloquent and passionate teacher, well-versed in Scripture but lacking a full understanding of the gospel. Instead of correcting him publicly or dismissing his effort, they pull him aside and teach him more accurately the way of Christ.

That moment, simple, private, and strategic, would multiply Apollos' impact. Priscilla didn't need to take over the message to influence the mission. She didn't seek the platform. She stewarded it. Her role as a stabilizer, teacher, and advocate for truth shaped the early church far more than history has fully recorded.

Priscilla and Aquila remind us that some of the most essential leadership thrives near purpose, not near power. It happens in the in-between, where ideas are sharpened, voices are developed, and mission takes shape. Their ability to support, clarify, and steward vision in partnership is not a lesser calling. It is a spiritually mature one. And it invites us to see leadership not as authorship, but as alignment with God's purpose in whatever seat we occupy.

You may not be the one who initiates the mission, but your care for how it unfolds may be the very thing that preserves its integrity. That is not a weakness. That is strength with wisdom. It is what it means to be called to implement.

Leadership in Real Life

How the Call Takes Shape in Everyday Leadership

Leadership from a vision-carrying lens is keenly attentive. These leaders hold institutional memory and relational equity. They're the ones who see the long game and help ensure that teams move forward with alignment, not just momentum. In many organizations, they lead from roles like chief of staff, church administrator, project director, or strategic operations manager. They're wired to help anchor execution, with care and foresight. And without them, even the best ideas and concepts collapse under pressure.

Have you ever left a meeting where everyone else celebrated the idea, while you quietly mapped the reality required to make it possible? This is the Carrier's lens. In a room full of endless enthusiasm, this foresight is often mislabeled as resistance or pessimism. But let me encourage you; clarity is not cynicism, it is courage. It is born from the discipline and gift of seeing things through to their conclusion, anticipating pitfalls, mapping out all who are needed at the table to collaborate, what resource gaps may be present, and ensuring the mission is built to last. This is stewardship at its core.

The Reward and the Responsibility

There is something deeply fulfilling about seeing a vision come to life, not because your name is attached to it, but because you know you helped it flourish. The reward comes in watching things work. The tension, however, is real. Carriers often bear the emotional labor of leadership while managing the magnitude that others don't see. If you're not careful, this can lead to depletion masked as diligence.

Sometimes you question the value of your unseen work. But the truth is, without people like you and the teams you surround yourself with, vision fades. Without people who understand systems, manage timing, and hold things steady, the best intentions can unravel.

That's why it's vital to anchor your worth in assignment, not acknowledgment. Implementing well requires wisdom and boundaries. You don't have to hold everything. You just have to hold what's yours and hold it faithfully.

Leading Whole

You lead whole when the quality of your work becomes your ultimate measure of success, not external validation. Your focus must be on the integrity of the offering itself. **The spiritual discipline of the Carrier is to ensure that every system, process, and document you produce meets an internal standard of excellence that transcends the job description.** Your administrative fidelity is a form of worship, regardless of who sees the final output.

So guard your strength. Build routines that replenish you rather than drain you. Practice telling yourself that commitment carries more weight than noise. And keep people around you who see your contribution clearly, who remind you that this kind of leadership is never hidden from God, even when humans overlook it.

When Priscilla opened her home, taught in private, and strengthened others without a pulpit, she showed us that legacy doesn't require limelight. It requires obedience. Lead whole, not just well.

Prayer

Father,

Thank You for calling me to this work. Help me to steward this season, this assignment, and this space with strength and humility.

When I'm tempted to reach for more than what You've given, remind me that obedience is the goal, not control.

When I grow weary, replenish my strength. When I doubt the value of what I implement, restore my vision.

Make me a leader who builds what lasts, not for recognition but for Your honor and glory.

Help me walk in step with others, honor the work that began before me, and advance it with courage and grace.

Amen.

Leadership Check-In

Pause and reflect on how this anchor meets your current season.

- What responsibility am I implementing right now that depends on my integrity to continue?
- Have I ever confused my proximity to purpose with the need to control or direct it?
- Where might I be holding something too tightly, and what would it look like to release it back to God?
- In what ways can I be more intentional about how I support, clarify, or guard vision with others? How can I lead well without trying to prove my worth?

The Steward's Seat

The Steward's Seat

The Steward's Seat

The Steward's Seat

Anchor #3

Calibrated
for Impact

The Steward's Seat

Anchor 3: Calibrated for Impact — The Gravity of Earned Influence

Leadership Reflection + Biblical Connection

There comes a point in a steward's journey when leadership stops being a job and starts becoming its own force of nature. A position may grant access, but it's your consistency, judgment, and character that make your presence impossible to ignore. Over time, your team stops listening to your official title and starts watching your posture. You aren't just making decisions but rather shaping the culture, setting the tone, and defining the truth for the room, whether you actively realize it or not.

This shift is the gravity of earned influence. It is not the influence you chase or demand, but the kind that settles upon you after years of showing up, making the hard calls, and prioritizing integrity when shortcuts beckon. This influence is born from a life lived under a spiritual contract. It is what forms when people have silently observed how you navigate pressure, how you respond to offense, and how you carry disappointment without letting it poison the mission. You didn't request this gravity, but it found you because your character created the space for it.

What makes this type of leadership so profound is that you don't just carry organizational strategy; you carry moral consequences. You are constantly weighing not only what is *possible*, but what is *right*. And that ability to choose the true path doesn't come from ambition; it comes from alignment. It flows from an inner life continually refined by three essential components:

- **Wisdom** provides the **compass**
- **Experience** provides the **context**
- **Discernment** provides the **timing**

Together, these three elements are the stewardship trinity. They help shape decisions that keep missions securely on course. When they are out of alignment, influence becomes volatile. But when they are aligned, they become a calm, internal force that holds things together.

This truth draws me to the story of Mordecai. He held no public office and carried no religious mantle, yet his influence changed the trajectory of an entire nation. His leadership wasn't forged in a palace. It was forged at the city gate, in the faithful proximity of his purpose. He was consistent, watchful, and rooted in his identity. When crisis hit, he didn't panic. He positioned.

When Haman's plot emerged, Mordecai didn't try to take matters into his own hands. He activated the influence he had already nurtured. He sent word to Esther with that piercing challenge, "*And who knows but that you have come to your royal position for such a time as this?*" (Esther 4:14). When was the last time your influence was needed for intervention instead of advancement?

This was not manipulation. It was a spiritual mirror. Mordecai didn't need to be the visionary to affirm the divine moment. His influence was pure because his motives were clear. He discerned the urgency, trusted Esther's place, and reminded her that influence is never given for self-preservation. It is always given for intervention. Mordecai's strength was in his restraint. He stayed in his lane, he fasted, and then he waited. He remained near the palace gate, close enough to be connected, yet far enough to remain grounded. This is the mark of a well-calibrated steward: knowing when to speak, when to release, and when to hold the space with wisdom instead of noise.

The gravity of your leadership today operates similarly. You may not hold the microphone, but your silence and presence speak volumes. Your glance across the table, your intentional pause before responding, your steady presence during tough times; all of it is being interpreted. When stewarded with this level of calibration, that influence will preserve what unwise choices and ambition might otherwise destroy.

Leadership in Real Life

How the Call Takes Shape in Everyday Leadership

Influence rarely makes a grand entrance. It is the small actions that stabilize, the moment of listening that invites deeper reflection that leads to new and innovative ideas, and the dependability when others are looking for an escape. Real influence is never demanded; it is simply observed.

I know we all have been there – in a meeting or board room where one leader can fill the discussion with frantic, unresearched solutions or ego-driven defensiveness. The steward, however, absorbs the initial chaos and waits until the storm passes. It is often the leader who absorbs the most information who ends up anchoring environments where confusion could or is used to dominate. You don't campaign for this kind of leadership. You become it through years of showing up with integrity, keen observation, and trust.

The Reward and the Responsibility

The reward of this mature influence is that you are entrusted with far more than tasks. You become the organization's stabilizer. People look at you not just for answers, but for unspoken cues. They read your silence more than you realize. This consistent faith in your emotional certainty is a profound reward.

This high level of trust, however, brings its own accountability. When your presence speaks before your mouth does, it creates constant, low-level pressure that others don't always see and one we rarely admit, so I'll just say it! This pressure is what I sometimes call the vigilance tax. You sometimes feel it as mental fatigue, emotional drain, and the continuous internal check: *Am I carrying a load that is mine to carry, or one that I was meant to release?* Being the one others rely on is honorable, but the internal absorption of organizational oversight, upkeep, and order requires intentional practices of replenishment. Your greatest energy is spent not on doing, but on being steady.

Leading Whole

To carry immense influence without collapsing beneath it, you must stay rooted in what is true. Your influence must flow from your identity as a beloved child of God, not from your insecurity or your professional credentials. This means you must prioritize your connection to the Divine above every other voice. It requires choosing humility when you could pull rank and releasing outcomes you cannot possibly control.

Leading whole means pouring into and mentoring others to carry influence well, too. You are not meant to be the sole anchor. Build capacity in others by teaching them what you've learned about timing, trust, and self-control. Give away the influence you've been given and watch others bloom, but also don't forget to be there when they need a shoulder to lean on or a thought partner along the way. When you lead whole, you don't just hold the line; you also multiply the impact across your entire organization.

Prayer

God, thank You for entrusting me with influence that is rooted in truth. Thank You for the wisdom and discernment that comes from walking closely with You.

I admit that life is overwhelming at times. I often see and sense things others may tend to miss. I feel the constant demand to speak, to pause, to lead with calibrated precision, and some days, it exhausts me.

Remind me that this is not a load to be carried alone. Remind me that every decision, every moment, every pivotal choice is first Yours before it is mine. Help me stay rooted in Your word. Help me to lead not from anxiety or control, but from calm alignment.

Teach me to honor the trust others have placed in me, not with fear, but with faithfulness. Let my influence be grounded in character. Help me to support the leaders above and beneath. Let it draw people toward clarity. Build in me the strength to carry what You've assigned me to carry, and the grace to release what is not mine. Amen.

Leadership Check-In

Use the following prompts for reflection, journaling, or conversation with a trusted mentor.

- Where is my influence showing up most strongly right now? Am I being intentional with the moral consequence I carry in that space?
- Thinking about the "trinity" of influence (Wisdom, Experience, Discernment), which one is currently my weakest link? What is one step I can take to calibrate it?
- How have I recently allowed the gravity of my presence (my look, my silence, my posture) to settle a room or guide a decision?
- Do I need to create more space in my rhythms to recover from the emotional vigilance I carry? What does releasing control look like for me in this season?

- What is one specific action I can take to mentor a team member to carry their *own* influence better? Am I hoarding responsibility or actively multiplying it?

_____

_____

_____

_____

_____

_____

_____

_____

_____

_____

_____

_____

_____

_____

_____

_____

_____

_____

_____

_____

_____

_____

_____

_____

_____

_____

_____

_____

_____

The Steward's Seat

The Steward's Seat

35

Anchor # 4

Humility in
High
Places

The Steward's Seat

Anchor 4: Humility in High Places: The Strength of a Grounded Heart

Leadership Reflection + Biblical Connection

Humility is one of the most misread virtues in leadership spaces. It's too often mistaken for weakness, indecision, or a lack of presence. But true humility in high places is none of those distortions. In fact, it is one of the most powerful postures a leader can carry, especially when you hold significant influence, visibility, or authority. Humility, rightly understood, is not about shrinking back or denying your gifts. It is about remaining grounded in the truth of who you are, who you serve, and what you've been entrusted with, particularly when the stakes are high, and eyes are on you.

As leaders climb the ladder of responsibility, its natural for the gravitational pull toward ego grows stronger. There are moments when applause feels good, when our opinions feel final, and when the rooms we walk into start to mirror the esteem others hold for us. It's human to feel it, but it's holy to resist it. For stewards, those who've been placed in seats of trust, this kind of humility is not optional. It is essential. Because the higher we go, the more rooted we must become. When your leadership has the power to impact systems, people, outcomes, and legacy, there must be something anchoring you beyond ambition or approval. That anchor is humility.

Scripture gives us a powerful and beautiful portrait of this through the life of Jesus. John 13 tells us that Jesus, fully aware of His authority and divinity, rose from the table, wrapped a towel around

His waist, and knelt to wash His disciples' feet. This was not the act of someone trying to prove their worth. **He was acting as someone completely secure in himself and his purpose.** That moment wasn't for validation. It was a declaration: *the greatest leaders do not lead to be seen; they lead to serve*. They understand that titles and power never exempt you from compassion and closeness. **Through this powerful act, Jesus was establishing the ultimate leadership principle for their future: true authority is servant leadership, and their governance was to be rooted in closeness and care.**

In today's leadership landscape, where many chase clout over calling, where we often witness the damage caused by those hungry for command but devoid of humility, humility becomes a rare but vital virtue. For stewards, it looks like taking responsibility without needing a nod or applause. It sounds like speaking up in truth when silence feels safer. It feels like recognizing that your strength comes not from controlling everything, but from releasing what you can and building up new anchors around you. Humility is not about thinking less of yourself but thinking of yourself accurately. It's leading with sober judgment, grounded confidence, and an unwavering commitment to serve what's right, not just what's impressive.

I have found that in those moments, I must force myself to return to the truth: The power flow originates elsewhere. I am a steward.

Leadership in Real Life

How the Call Takes Shape in Everyday Leadership

If no one has ever told you this, let me be the first - Humility is an active practice of personal and spiritual surrender. It requires strength to listen fully before responding. It takes maturity to acknowledge limits, not because you're weak, but because you're wise. It demands sensitivity to not ask, "Will this make me look good?" but rather "Will this honor the assignment I've been entrusted with?" Humility means you are willing to embrace the learning process, letting others teach you, and being secure enough to let someone else be right. This posture builds profound trust in others.

The Reward and the Responsibility

The reward of humility in leadership is profound internal security. It builds a confidence rooted not in being right, but in pursuing what is truly right. You grow resilient to criticism and applause alike, anchored in your assignment.

The consequence, however, is that high-level arrogance and pride can poison an entire team faster than almost any other I know. When the steward confuses their seat with their identity, trust dissolves. Humility is the shield that can protect the mission from the leader's own human flaws. It creates space for others to contribute, making the mission stronger than any single person.

Leading Whole

To lead whole, you must remember that humility begins within long before it's seen outside. Humility is recognizing who you are and who you are not. It is the release of proving, performing, and carrying loads you were never meant to hold alone. When you stop equating your worth with how well you hold everything together or what others will rate you on their invisible expectation scale, you create space for God to actually be God. This is where whole leadership begins: acknowledging limits as trust, not defeat.

Jesus showed us what this looks like. He did not serve from depletion or insecurity, but from a rooted identity. With full authority, He chose to serve. With fullness, He bowed. His humility was not self-reduction but alignment. And even Jesus, who carried complete authority, experienced moments of heaviness. Remember in the garden He asked for the cup to pass. That was a real moment of pure honesty. **Isn't it a comfort to know that even He showed us just how human and weighty life can feel at times?** Nevertheless, He returned to the Father. In prayer, He was strengthened. In communion, He was steadied. He rose from that place renewed, clear, and ready to continue the mission before Him.

Leading whole means returning to the Source in the same way. You do not serve to prove your capacity or earn identity. You serve from a heart that is held, nourished, and continually realigned. The call is not to lead without weariness, but to bring your weariness back to God and be restored. Only a grounded and replenished heart can carry leadership with grace.

Prayer

God, thank you for the privilege of leadership. I know that every open door, every decision I face, and every voice I steward is a reflection of your trust in me. Help me to never take that lightly. Remind me that influence is not for show but service.

Teach me to lead with wisdom, not ego. May I carry this role with reverence, recognizing that you've called me not just to lead, but to reflect your heart in how I lead.

When I am praised, keep me grounded. When I am overlooked, keep me steady. When decisions are hard, keep me wise. And when I feel overwhelmed, remind me that I do not lead alone. Thank you for modeling what true humility looks like. Help me walk in your footsteps, not for applause, but for purpose.

In Jesus' name, Amen.

Leadership Check-In

Take a quiet moment to reflect on where your leadership is being stretched, tested, or refined. Use the prompts below to journal your thoughts and revisit your posture as a steward.

- What decision or responsibility am I currently carrying that requires me to willingly submit to a better idea (even if it wasn't mine)?
- In what area of my leadership have I recently confused my *capacity* with my *identity*?
- How am I actively creating space for others to contribute and gain credit, rather than letting my stature dominate the room?
- What does humility look like for me right now in this specific season, with this specific assignment I carry?
- Where might God be inviting me to lead with vulnerability (asking for help or admitting a limit) instead of needing to be right?

The Steward's Seat

The Steward's Seat

Anchor # 5

Leading from the Middle

Anchor 5: Leading from the Middle: The Integrity of the In-Between

Leadership Reflection + Biblical Connection

Leading from the middle is a rare and powerful form of leadership. But what does leading from the middle really mean? It's the person(s) who acts as the essential operational and relational link between vision and execution. You are close enough to see the top but grounded enough to understand and have a real connection with what's beneath. You interpret vision, mediate conflict, and sometimes have to carry what didn't always start with you but still relies on you. You are both a bridge and a buffer, trusted and tested, pulled in multiple directions while expected to remain steady. And the higher the stakes, the more the magnitude of your value can become unseen.

Yet this is where some of the most transformative leadership happens. By influencing how vision lives beyond the meeting and holding the pulse of the people, you shape outcomes. This is the environment where you wield true operational authority. It is a vital position of trust, deep ethical insight, and unparalleled strategic worth.

There is also something deeply spiritual about occupying this space. Middle leaders are called to live in what I like to call *Upward Honor, Downward Care*: honoring and supporting authority above while protecting and shaping capacity below. It requires emotional fluency, political awareness, and a discerning spirit that knows how to move between rooms without losing your center. You often see the cracks before anyone else does, carry the unspoken difficulties, and manage expectations while translating what's aspirational into something achievable. This essential work is often done in the shadows, without the fanfare, and sometimes without the full context.

The life of Jonathan, son of Saul, is one of Scripture's clearest examples of this kind of leadership. Positioned between a king and a future king, he bore the load of loyalty and transition. His father was deteriorating as a leader, his friend David was emerging as God's chosen successor, and Jonathan was caught in the middle, honoring one, protecting the other, and leading with conviction.

Jonathan had every natural right to the throne, yet he surrendered it without bitterness. That surrender was not weakness. It was wisdom. It takes deep spiritual confidence to say, "I see what God is doing, and I will not stand in the way of it, even if it costs me position or acknowledgment." Using his position for the kingdom's sake rather than his own gain, he risked his life to protect David. His speaking of hard truths to Saul carried the risk of shattering their relationship. Despite this conflict, he stood amid the crosscurrents of divided loyalties and never let it divide his integrity. That kind of leadership may not always be visible on the surface, but it sustains the people, preserves the mission, and protects the future. Jonathan was not an interim. He was an intercessor, someone who stood in the middle and held space with wisdom and loyalty until the next season could arrive.

Many of us are called to that same posture. We subtly adjust, recalibrate, redirect, and rebuild so that the mission stays intact. Middle leadership is sacred because it is sacrificial. And like Jonathan, we are called to discern what God is doing, honor the leaders around us, speak the truth in love, and steward the season with open hands and a guarded heart. You are helping secure legacy. And in heaven's eyes, that is leadership of the highest kind.

Leadership in Real Life

How the Call Takes Shape in Everyday Leadership

Leading from the middle is the ultimate test of emotional fluency. You are tasked with *simultaneous translation*: you must manage the visionary language of the executive while interpreting that into the practical, achievable practice for the people you lead. You are constantly operating between two different realities and must ensure the entire structure remains functional and aligned.

This simultaneous translation requires specific practices to manage the flow of vision. There are many, but here are three that I have embraced and learned to adopt:

- **Practice 1: The Current State Diagnostic**. Before moving forward with an aspirational command, first analyze the current state posture to determine if the enabling components are present. The actionable step is often building the tools/resources necessary to realize the vision/goal, rather than immediately executing the goal itself.
- **Practice 2: Grounding the Vision**. When confronted with a broad, ambiguous, or highly conceptual goal, your immediate action should be to translate abstract language into concrete, measurable steps. This means breaking the vision down into perhaps 2 to 3 future state desired outcomes, ensuring each has a clear owner and a defined delivery date. This provides immediate stability for your team, protects against confusion, and defines the clear, executable critical path for success.
- **Practice 3: Model Confidence**. Most organizations pull toward informality and speed. Your job is to pull it back to structure. Model the reserved strength of a steward who trusts the process. Not every situation will be the same, requiring

you to flex based on the state of play, but overall, your steadiness becomes the structural reference point for everyone else.

The Reward and the Responsibility

The reward is the unwavering *moral assurance*. You gain the internal peace of knowing your character and your calling are aligned. This self-replenishing identity is the profound payoff: knowing that your steady sacrifice is actively securing the future. You earn the internal stature that no title can grant, and your success is measured by the enduring health and clarity of the systems and people you serve.

The responsibility, however, is the sustained weight of stewardship. Leading from the middle often requires holding context others simply do not see, carrying knowledge that cannot always be shared, and absorbing pressure. You become a stabilizing force while protecting people from unnecessary disruption. The cost is not the temptation to misuse power, but the discipline to remain steady when outcomes take time to reveal themselves.

This role demands patience, restraint, and a long view. The responsibility of the middle leader is not to dominate the structure, but to hold it together. That kind of faithfulness requires endurance, emotional maturity, and a deep commitment to something larger than personal validation. This is not weakness. It is strength under control. And it is the quiet courage that keeps institutions healthy and futures intact.

Leading Whole

To lead whole is to recognize that surrender is the key to endurance. Jonathan surrendered the position to secure the greater purpose. Leading whole means you refuse to lose your center, even when pulled in multiple directions. It requires creating pauses for prayer and reflection to discern which responsibility is truly yours to carry, and which belongs to God, your team, or your principal. Your worth is not defined by the seat you occupy, but by the structural integrity with which you serve the assignment.

Prayer

God, I thank you for the sacred responsibility of middle leadership. Thank you for trusting me with this seat, not because I have all the answers, but because you've ordered my steps to stand in hard places with humility, strength, and wisdom.

Help me to lead like Jonathan, with a heart that honors authority, a spirit that discerns your will, and a posture that protects what matters. Teach me how to navigate complex dynamics with patience, to speak truth with grace, and to guard the mission.

When I feel caught between competing voices, remind me that you are the one voice I can always trust. When I feel unseen, remind me that you see me. And when the charge feels too heavy, remind me that I am never carrying it alone.

Let my leadership reflect your character. Let my presence bring stability. Let my words bring clarity. And let my discernment preserve what is good, even when others don't yet see the risk. I surrender the need to be known and ask instead to be effective, faithful, and aligned with your purpose.

Make me a faithful steward of the in-between. Use my voice to build bridges. Use my judgment to safeguard vision. And use my hands to serve wherever you place me, confident not in position, but in the calling you have entrusted.

In Jesus' name, Amen.

The Steward's Seat

Leadership Check-In

Take a moment to sit and reflect on your current leadership role. Think honestly on the dilemmas you are holding, the clarity you need, and the reserved strength you bring to spaces that may not always see your full impact.

- Where am I currently being stretched between two roles, two people, or two outcomes?
- How have I been stewarding my influence privately, even when I haven't been publicly acknowledged?
- What does it look like for me to speak truth in a way that preserves both relationships and integrity?
- In what ways is God asking me to surrender position to protect purpose?
- Am I leading with humility like Jonathan, or striving to be heard instead of trusting the assignment?

The Steward's Seat

The Steward's Seat

The Steward's Seat

The Steward's Seat

Anchor #6

Wisdom Over Impulse

Anchor 6: Wisdom Over Impulse — The Sacred Discipline of the Pause

Leadership Reflection + Biblical Connection

We all know that there is a difference between being decisive and being reactive. Leadership often demands timely decisions, clear direction, and confident action, but a vital line exists between leading with focus and leading from a place of internal pressure. The true test of leadership isn't speed; it's the discipline to assess before acting.

When I talk about leading in a rush, I'm not referring to emotional outbursts or visible chaos. More often, rushing shows up as *premature decisiveness*. It can sound like wrapping up a discussion before all perspectives are surfaced, making decisions before the full picture is clear, or moving forward simply because momentum is demanding it. This kind of internal urgency can feel responsible, even prudent, but wisdom often requires creating space rather than accelerating the moment. Over-functioning where a pause would serve you introduces avoidable risk, misalignment, and downstream correction. Rushing interrupts the process to fully assess, shortcuts listening, and prioritizes resolution over full visibility and clarity. **Always remember that the higher your level of responsibility, the more costly that trade-off becomes**.

Wisdom pauses. It hears what's unsaid and filters urgency through discernment. Intentional action is the main goal. This kind of leadership draws strength not from how fast you move, but from how well you see and hear. Measured speech, strategic pause, and movement guided by experience and insight mark this posture rather than ego or fear.

The story of Solomon, one of my favorites, has always grounded this truth for me. In 1 Kings 3, when Solomon first assumes the throne, God offers him an open invitation to ask for anything. He could have asked for military power or territorial gain, but he asked for wisdom: for a perceptive heart to govern the people well. That single request shows real leadership: seeking the power to discern truth, not the illusion of it. Solomon didn't pray for the appearance of wisdom; he prayed for the ***actual ability to weigh what is true***.

Not long after, he was tested. Two women came before him, both claiming to be the mother of the same infant. With no witnesses or evidence, the moment required more than positional authority; it required spiritual perception. Solomon's surprising response, proposing to divide the child in two, was not cruelty; accuracy was the aim he was looking to uncover. This approach forced the *true mother* to reveal herself, not through logic, but through unconditional love. Solomon saw the truth through the true motivation of her heart. He demonstrated what wisdom under pressure looks like. The kingdom took notice. Trust was established by restraint and revelation.

That story reminds me that leadership will always bring moments when the facts feel clear as mud and trust must be paired with verification. Mastering the line between focus and reaction is the relentless work of leadership. But the Spirit is faithful to check us, nudging us toward pause, reminding us that restraint is not weakness, but rather wisdom in motion. When leaders step into a high-stakes scenario, the first move should be an internal one: pausing long enough to ask, "*Am I about to lead from wisdom or from unwise speed? What's guiding the next move? Fear, ego, fatigue, or the Spirit?*" Sometimes the wisest leadership action is simply asking for a moment to process. **There is power in the pause**.

Leadership in Real Life

How the Call Takes Shape in Everyday Leadership

Choosing wisdom over impulse is a daily act of steering action with purpose. As a steward, you are often the one standing between speed and the operational reality, and your role is to ensure alignment.

The steward operates as the essential buffer in high-stakes moments. Your function is not to constantly veto without insight or direction, but to provide the governance and framework that enable effective action. This requires strategic restraint. Instead of matching enthusiasm with immediate pushback, the steward secures a reserved time for comprehensive analysis. This pause enables you to filter momentum through metrics, resource availability, and the potential toll on the team's capacity. The goal of this restraint is not stagnation, but calibration. It ensures that moments are met with preparation and a roadmap of reality. This posture protects the integrity of the mission, models what spiritual leadership looks like in a professional setting and deepens trust with authority.

The Reward and the Responsibility

When you model restraint, the reward is the substance of your word. When you say, "*Let me think on this*," people trust the answer you bring back because it is rooted in intentionality. This is the stature established not by grand pronouncements, but by the certainty of your decision-making.

But what happens when you don't have time to be overtly thoughtful? This is where the prior discipline pays off. If you are ever forced to respond immediately, you must rely on the internal certainty forged during your history of experiences, wisdom, and knowledge. This means leading with the highest ethical commitment and operational insight available in the moment, trusting the preparation of your heart and mind to guide your words. You may not have time for a strategic pause in the moment, but a pattern of restraint ensures your response is rooted in truth and the best facts available, not driven by impulse.

The flip side is the responsibility of being the one who provides reflection and restraint. Stewards are uniquely wired to see the forest through the trees; you resist the urge to react, knowing that a short-term, temporary sacrifice of speed ensures a longer-term foundation of integrity and sturdier ground. The discipline required to acquire wisdom is immense. When leaders model that kind of posture, they create a culture where focus can thrive, and trust can grow.

Leading Whole

To lead whole means governing yourself before governing others. Ask God not just for insight into any situation, but spiritual insight into your own heart. The maturity to acknowledge that your frustration, exhaustion, fear, or even ego can be the biggest source of impatience is required. This is why the Bible calls us to *crucify the flesh daily* (Galatians 5:24). While this command is often applied to moral struggles, its leadership application is also profound. If we don't tend to our *internal ground*, how can we possibly hear God clearly in the moment of decision? Lead whole by building the pause into your day. Sometimes it's praying silently mid-meeting. Sometimes it's asking a question that reframes the entire discussion. It could also look like going for a walk to get fresh air or shutting your office door just to stand still in silence for a little while. The wisest thing you can often do is *ask for space to reflect*. Wisdom over impulse means we refuse to make decisions from turbulence. The true measure of leadership is not just what we know, but in how we steward what we know.

Prayer

God Thank You for being the steady guide in a world that moves way too fast. In moments when my internal urge to react is to prove, or to speak too quickly, anchor me in the kind of perception that listens before it leads. Help me to recognize the hallowed pause, the moments between stimulus and response, where Your Spirit speaks loudest.

Give me a heart that chooses understanding over urgency. Let my words be rooted in truth, not pride. Teach me to read between the lines in every conversation and to sense when Your wisdom is calling me to wait.

When I feel the need to defend myself, settle me in the truth that You are my defender. When others move quickly, remind me that I do not have to match their pace to stay aligned with Your purpose.

Father, I ask for a perceptive heart like Solomon's. Not just to govern others, but to govern myself. Help me sift through emotion, opinion, and distraction so that what comes from my mouth is life-giving, timely, and right. Let my restraint reflect maturity, not fear. Let my insight reflect intimacy with You.

Help me steward the moments I'm given, especially the ones that call for precision in uncertainty. And when I do speak, may my words carry truth. Let my leadership mirror Yours: full of mercy, full of patience, and always full of wisdom.

In Jesus' name, Amen.

Leadership Check-In

Take a moment to pause. Sit with the places in your leadership where you feel the pressure to respond quickly, speak first, or prove you're in control. Let this moment be a pause and an invitation to listen

69

deeper than the noise and remember that wisdom often waits before it speaks.

This is not about shrinking your voice. It's about centering your voice in spiritual insight. Leadership in today's world is filled with noise, urgency, and pressure to perform. Spiritual leadership calls for a kind of listening that isn't just about ears, but about spirit. It calls for restraint that comes from conviction.

You are not called to match the pace of the crowd. You are called to move at the pace of truth.

- Where in my leadership do I feel pressure to speak or act quickly, even when I'm not fully clear?
- Have I made recent decisions from a place of reaction instead of revelation?
- What does it practically look like for me to lead with wisdom over the urge to react in this season?
- Where is God inviting me to pause, to ask for understanding, and to speak only when it is time?

_____
_____
_____
_____
_____
_____
_____
_____
_____
_____
_____
_____

The Steward's Seat

The Steward's Seat

The Steward's Seat

Anchor #7
Guarding
Vision in the
Gaps

Anchor 7: Guarding Vision in the Gaps — The Integrity of Preservation

Leadership Reflection + Biblical Connection

Every mission faces moments of vulnerability. Sometimes, those moments come in the form of opposition. But more often, they arrive slowly through misalignment, organizational drift, misplaced urgency and priority, or the watering down of a once-strong vision. And it is in these moments that stewards are called to protect, preserve, and uphold what others may not fully see.

There are seasons in leadership when you're not simply advancing the plan, but simultaneously guarding the soul of it. You may find yourself tracing back to what was originally declared and weighing whether the current direction still aligns with the original call. You may not be the author of the original mission statement, but you serve as the curator of its health, ensuring its foundational integrity is preserved. You are the vital administrative link ensuring the original mandate endures and is passed along, complete and whole to the next generation.

This is not about control but conviction. And it's one of the highest forms of stewardship.

Nehemiah's story teaches this in profound ways. While many remember him as a master wall-builder, I see him as the ultimate vision protector. His leadership began not in Jerusalem, but in the Persian palace, where he held the position of cupbearer to King Artaxerxes. Nehemiah was an Israelite, serving within a powerful, secular government, yet his steps were divinely ordered for a purpose much greater than his daily job description. This placement shows us a powerful truth: sometimes, God strategically positions His stewards in foreign environments. Like corporate offices, government systems, board rooms, etc., because that is where the influence is needed most. Nehemiah's heart remained anchored to his people and their original mission, even while his hands worked for the King of Persia. This *intentional placement* was the foundation for his future leadership.

When Nehemiah finally presented his request to King Artaxerxes, God demonstrated His sovereign strategy. The King, entirely unaware of the divine significance of Jerusalem's walls, had his heart stirred by God. Not only did he grant Nehemiah leave, but he also provided official royal decrees, timber from the king's forest, and military protection for the journey. This is a profound lesson: ***God uses the resources and authority of the very systems we serve, often moving leaders around us to execute His purpose***. Nehemiah didn't just lead a construction project. He guarded the integrity of a divine assignment that had been delayed, dismissed, and diluted. He stepped into a story that began well before him, yet treated the call with the same vital gravity as if it had been given directly to him.

When Nehemiah heard about the broken walls of Jerusalem, he didn't jump into action immediately. He wept. He fasted. He prayed. He sat with the assignment long before he shared it. And when he finally stepped into leadership, he did so with one hand on the work and one hand on spiritual insight. He was managing the workforce while filtering every decision through what God originally intended for His people.

It didn't take long for the mission to come under pressure from external threats, internal discouragement, manipulative alliances, and false prophets. Nehemiah faced them all just like we experience in today's world. At every turn, there were opportunities to compromise, to soften the assignment, or to allow urgency or emotion to detour direction. But he didn't bend.

In one of the most defining moments, Nehemiah is invited multiple times to meet with opposing leaders under the guise of diplomacy, but he saw through the trap. And his response is one that every steward needs in their leadership vocabulary: *"I am doing a great work, and I cannot come down."*

He understood that distraction in a vulnerable moment could destroy the very thing God had asked him to do and protect. That's the kind of posture required to guard vision in the gap between what's been declared and what's being delivered.

The ultimate testament to Nehemiah's leadership and God's favor was the completion of the entire wall in just fifty-two days. This incredible speed and efficiency proved the mission was divinely blessed and silenced their external opposition. The wall's completion proved that integrity and adherence to the blueprint overcome every obstacle.

Leadership in Real Life

How the Call Takes Shape in Everyday Leadership

So much of our modern leadership culture celebrates momentum, but without alignment, it can be disruptive and even dangerous. A fast-moving team with no compass doesn't build legacy; it burns itself out chasing motion. Stewards, especially those second in command, are often the only ones close enough to the ground and the top to sense when something is off.

Your role is to be the living memory of the mission, holding the historical blueprint when the room is captivated by a new, exciting initiative. You are the organization's barometer, using past lessons to prevent repeated mistakes and lay firmer ground for the future. This means you function as the integrity filter. Your role isn't to block progress but rather anchor it. By asking sharp, principled questions, you redirect focus: *Does this new direction honor our foundational values? Are we sacrificing our long-term mandate for a short-term win?* This refocusing back to the values is the very essence of preservation leadership.

The Reward and the Responsibility

When you guard vision, the reward is the internal stature of knowing you protected the mission's integrity from mutation. What exactly does that mutation look like? It often manifests as a subtle compromise: sacrificing quality assurance steps just to meet an arbitrarily aggressive deadline; shifting foundational values to chase a new trend; or tolerating an employee's toxic behavior for the sake of short-term output. This last compromise is one of the most critical because undoubtedly, the greatest area of mission preservation is the team itself. People rarely see organizational tolerance for toxicity as an erosion of vision, yet when you allow the core of your culture to rot, the mission cannot stand. You gain moral authority when you refuse to let the mission become a cheaper, easier version of its intended self. The fulfillment comes from ensuring that the mission, decades from now, will still reflect the original, uncompromising purpose.

Defending the mission comes at a cost, often mistaken for rigidity or lost momentum. You may bear the toll of having to endure the crosscurrents of differing loyalties, speaking "not yet" when others want a "yes." I encourage you to stand watch and hold the line, not because you want power, but because you fear the consequence that follows unfaithful stewardship. You stay close because it is better to endure the dilemma of speaking up than to let the mission fade away in silence.

Leading Whole

To lead whole while guarding what's been assigned to you means building the *"I cannot come down"* conviction into your own personal practice. This is not just a boundary you set with the outside world, but rather an internal law you establish for yourself. Leading begins with self-governance. Your inner state, whether anxious or steady, sets the tone for the team. Guarding the mission requires you to guard your own focus. You must be disciplined about what noise and distraction you allow into your personal life. When you feel the internal urge to justify, defend, or join a detour, you must anchor yourself in Nehemiah's words. The refusal to come down also means setting a spiritual boundary around your time, your emotional reserves, and your priorities. This practice demands proactive self-stewardship: You pray for insight. You listen for what's not being said. You appropriately say "not yet" when others want a yes right away. You remember the gravity of what was entrusted. This commitment to self-governance is the true foundation of preservation leadership, ensuring that your greatest influence flows from a sustained and protected source.

Prayer

Father,

You are the Author of vision and the Keeper of purpose. You see the fracture before it spreads, the drift before it derails, the misalignments before they become visible divides. And still, You call me to stand in the gap, to watch and to listen.

Help me, Lord, to be a faithful steward of what You have called me to protect. Not just the tasks, but the truth behind them. Teach me how to hold crosscurrents without becoming hard. Show me how to preserve alignment without stepping into arrogance. Let my caution not be seen as fear, but as reverence. Let my voice not be reactive but rooted in stability.

Give me the courage to ask the right questions, even if I'm the only one asking them. Give me the wisdom to know when to pause and when to push forward. Help me embrace the vision enough to protect it and care for the people enough to guide them gently back when we've wandered.

Let me be like Nehemiah, willing to build and battle at the same time. Willing to finish the wall, not just start it. Willing to name what's not aligned; not to shame, but to restore.

And when I feel unseen or misunderstood, remind me that You see. And You honor faithfulness in the gap. Amen.

Leadership Check-In

Take a moment to reflect on where you may be the last line of defense for a mission, a moment, or a message that is at risk of being reshaped by speed or silence. Ask yourself what needs guarding and what needs grounding.

- Where in my leadership environment do I sense a drift from the original vision or values?
- Have I grown numb to small misalignments because they feel too hard to address?
- What does it look like to protect the mission without positioning myself as the "vision police"?
- Am I asking the hard questions behind closed doors or avoiding them to keep the peace?
- How can I become a steady presence in this season?
- What is God asking me to watch over right now, and am I alert?

The Steward's Seat

Anchor #8

Boundaries and Renewal

Anchor 8: Boundaries and Renewal — The Mandate of Self-Stewardship

Leadership Reflection + Biblical Connection

In leadership, there is a powerful myth that drives many leaders: the belief that you must be perpetually available to keep this purpose running. Because your role is so vital in translating vision, filtering, and safeguarding operational health, it's easy to confuse dedication with personal capacity. This mindset makes you the anchor, but it can also quickly make you the *weakest link*. The internal committed turbulence you absorb and the feeling that you must constantly hold the line can lead directly to burnout. It clouds your judgement and steals the joy that once fueled you.

Your first act of stewardship is governing your own capacity. Renewal is not a reward you earn after the work is done, but it's the discipline that ensures you can finish the race. This has been one of the most transformative principles I've learned in recent years, and I am still learning to live it. It is incredibly difficult with the constant swirling of change, ideas, demands, and needs, but it is so necessary for leadership longevity. And every time I actually make room to pause, that's when the *sharpest insights and clearest direction surface.*

The most profound example of boundaries in leadership is the life of Jesus. Though He carried a world-altering mission and operated with inexhaustible power, He constantly modeled intentional withdrawal. When crowds pressed in, when disciples pushed for more, when needs multiplied faster than miracles, Jesus often pulled back. The gospels are filled with these moments: "*He would often withdraw to lonely places and pray*" (Luke 5:16). We see this pattern repeated: after a long day of healing and teaching (Mark 1:35); before choosing the twelve apostles (Luke 6:12); and immediately after miraculously feeding the five thousand (Mark 6:46).

That steady refrain—*He often withdrew*—is the leadership blueprint. For someone in your seat, it's not a footnote. It's the strategy. And it reinforced two truths:

1. **The Natural Implication (Boundaries):** The act of pulling back established a physical boundary, showing that divine power did not exempt His human body from fatigue or the need for sustained, protected focus. He refused to let the urgency of the moment violate the priority of His relationship with the Father.

2. **The Spiritual Implication (Reliance):** When He withdrew to pray, He was making a powerful declaration that every steward needs to hear: My ability to lead comes from My reliance on the Father, not from My human stamina. He protected His source. His boundaries were the visible manifestation of His humility and trust.

Jesus's example shows that withdrawal is not a failure of capacity. It is evidence of spiritual wisdom. Discipline requires establishing clear boundaries and choosing to walk away from demands (when you can) to protect your internal margin. True stewardship requires managing our personal energy with the same precision as we manage our organizations. We must choose to lead from a place of *being* rather than constant *doing*, trusting that the purpose belongs to God.

Leadership in Real Life

How the Call Takes Shape in Everyday Leadership

Renewal can come in countless forms. It's rarely a grand vacation, but that helps too! More often, it's a small, personal buffer you build into your rhythm. The steward must treat this space as a non-negotiable line item on their personal spreadsheet. This means guarding your calendar, meditation, prayer time, vacations, no-fly zones, family time, self-care, etc., against encroachment and refusing to let availability (*capacity*) become accountability (*obligation*).

The internal conflict is real. You may find yourself saying "yes" to keep the peace, believing it's easier to do the work than to set the boundary. This is where we tend to confuse service with self-neglect. When you start to notice that your default response is becoming more layered in cynicism, when minor inconveniences spark an overreaction, or when the joy of the project feels nowhere in sight, these are signals that your spirit is running on an empty tank. A boundary is a simple declaration: "*I honor my limits so I can honor my assignment.*"

The Reward and the Responsibility

The reward of prioritizing renewal is long-term viability. You gain internal confidence and strength in knowing you are leading sustainably, not frantically. Renewal sharpens your insight, restores your perspective, and makes you far more effective in high-stakes moments. You swap stress for stability.

The responsibility is the personal discipline required to set boundaries that others may not like or understand. When you function as an organizational anchor, saying "no," "not yet," "I need time to think about this", "I'll get to this when I can", or even "I need a break" can feel like a betrayal of trust. But this is where you have to stand firm. The most powerful gift you can offer those you lead is the preservation of your ability to lead them over the long haul.

Leading Whole

To lead whole means recognizing that your personal limits are not a flaw in your design. Think of it as a feature of your humanity. Your assignment is not a test of your personal strength but a reflection of God's trust. **You cannot steward the purpose well if you are not stewarding yourself well first.**

Lead whole by building deliberate pauses into your weekly practice. Guard your solitude, your prayer, and your rest with the same seriousness you guard your most critical assignment. Ask yourself, what is the one boundary I need to set in this season that will make me a more sustainable leader? Your greatest act of obedience might be simply choosing to rest, trusting that the work will wait, and knowing that the Father desires your restoration above your exhaustion.

Prayer

Father,

Thank You for modeling intentional rest and for reminding me that my endurance does not come from my own strength, but from You. I confess that I often fall into the trap of self-reliance, believing I must carry things alone. Yet Your word says, "*My grace is sufficient for you, for my power is made perfect in weakness.*" (2 Corinthians 12:9). Help me not to confuse my identity with my output.

Teach me to lead whole. Give me the spiritual insight to recognize the signals of fatigue and the courage to set boundaries when I need to be restored. Help me protect my practice of rest and solitude, knowing that this is an act of faithfulness to You, not a luxury for myself.

Anchor me in the truth that my worth is not defined by how much I accomplish, but by how faithfully I steward what You have given me. I surrender my need for constant activity and what seems the world's constant demand for it, embracing the wisdom of the pause.

Restore my soul, renew my vision, and let my leadership flow from Your well of living water. As the deer that pants for water, let my soul long for You above all else.

In Jesus' name, Amen.

Leadership Check-In

- What organizational or relational challenges are currently draining me most?
- Am I treating rest as a reward (something I earn) or as discipline (something I must practice)?
- What is the one non-negotiable boundary I need to establish in my calendar (personal and professional) to create mental and spiritual margin?
- How can I better communicate to my team that self-stewardship is a mandatory value, not a permission slip?
- What does genuine, non-productive rest look like for me right now, and am I willing to pursue it?

_____
_____
_____
_____
_____
_____

The Steward's Seat

The Steward's Seat

Anchor #9

Loyalty
with
Integrity

Anchor 9: Loyalty with Integrity — The Uncompromising Standard

Leadership Reflection + Biblical Connection

Integrity is the internal contract that truly matters in leadership. We commit to a role, a company, and a purpose, but for a leader anchored in faith, that commitment is always subject to a higher standard of truth. Yes, you manage the organization's resources, but you are ultimately beholden to the foundational principles that shape all truth.

The true test of a faithful leader is not whether you can be compliant, but whether you can maintain your moral standard when expediency or internal/external demands can compromise. The conflict often lands squarely on the shoulders of the person in your position and others. Protecting the assignment's ethical foundation requires a willingness to defend an uncomfortable truth.

True fidelity is not blind silence. It is the ability to honor the assignment while staying absolutely true to the ethical standards you profess. Never fall into the trap of thinking you must sacrifice your moral compass to achieve professional objectives. That is not effective leadership. That is a compromise.

The Old Testament gives us a powerful demonstration of this through Shadrach, Meshach, and Abednego. These three men were high-capacity stewards and elite administrators trusted within the Babylonian government. Their service demonstrated competence and rcliability.

But then came the test: King Nebuchadnezzar demanded that all leaders bow to a golden idol. This order was not a professional request, but an ethical and spiritual mandate that directly contradicted their core truth. They understood that bowing was not a small act of compliance, but a fundamental betrayal of their vertical commitment.

Their response to the King, found in Daniel 3:17-18, is one of the greatest declarations of leadership integrity ever recorded. They were respectful, clear, and firm: "*O Nebuchadnezzar, we do not need to answer you in this matter... our God whom we serve is able to deliver us... But if not, let it be known to you, O king, that we will not serve your gods or worship the golden image that you have set up.*"

Their faithfulness was active courage. When commanded to bow, they refused, choosing obedience to God over compliance with power, even when the consequence was death. That refusal led them directly into the fiery furnace, a punishment meant to destroy them publicly. Yet God met them there. They were not consumed by the fire because the presence of God stood with them in the flames. In response, the king *openly* praised their God, declaring that no other god could have delivered in this way. He immediately issued a decree protecting their worship and warning against speaking against the God they served. Their integrity did not just preserve their lives; it forced earthly authority to acknowledge divine power. This is the mandate for every leader who carries influence today. Integrity is not optional; it is the assignment.

Leadership in Real Life

How the Call Takes Shape in Everyday Leadership

Integrity today shows up in everyday ethical decisions. Ethical leadership requires asking hard questions when others may prefer the easy path. It can even look like refusing to endorse a report or budget that relies on inaccurate data.

This is where your professional conduct is refined. You must choose to defend the values of the assignment, especially when external pressure or internal norms or expediency threaten to erode them. This is the difference between a subordinate who simply follows orders and a steward who preserves the ethical foundation of the purpose. Where are you being asked to choose expediency over internal conviction?

The Reward and the Responsibility

The reward of standing on truth is moral freedom. When you lead with clean hands, you gain unshakeable confidence that no promotion can grant, and no demotion can take away. It's best to ensure your stature is rooted in your *character*, not in your current *position*.

And let's be brutally honest, standing on truth can bring about potential conflict, but that's a natural part of the responsibility we all must carry. Defending the ethical baseline requires courage and may involve experiencing relational bumps or professional isolation. This difficult reality reminds me of a truth I shared with the graduates of Charleston Southern University in the May of 2025 Commencement Ceremony: *"You will find yourself in environments where your convictions will be tested, and where silence will feel safer than truth. Show up anyway. Courage isn't the absence of fear; it's the presence of conviction when fear is loudest in your head."*

You must manage the very real fear that your integrity will be misinterpreted or viewed as inflexibility. This is where your private practice of faith is tested, proving that you fear God more than you fear professional censure.

Leading Whole

To lead whole means recognizing that your personal moral footing is the greatest asset you bring to the assignment. Protecting that compass is non-negotiable. You prepare for the test of integrity long before it arrives by covering your private life with truth.

Lead whole by recognizing that you have a spiritual responsibility to the people you serve. When a moment of confrontation is necessary, choose truth, but deliver it with Upward Honor, Downward Care. Your goal should not be to prove yourself right. It is to ensure the ethical health of the entire purpose.

Prayer

Father,

Thank You for setting a standard of truth that is higher than any earthly contract. I confess to the temptation to choose silence when truth is costly. Forgive me for confusing safety with integrity and prioritizing the approval of man over the will of God.

Grant me the courage to lead like Shadrach, Meshach, and Abednego; respectful, firm, and uncompromising when essential truth is challenged. Give me the wisdom to know when to speak, when to support, and when to refuse what is morally wrong.

Teach me to deliver hard truths, motivated by love for the leader and devotion to the larger purpose. Shield me from the fear of conflict and the fear of man and anchor my identity solely in Your approval. I choose loyalty with integrity today.

In Jesus' name, Amen.

Leadership Check-In

- Where in my current leadership dynamics am I tempted to choose silence just to keep the peace?
- What am I aware of that requires me to speak truth and defend integrity?
- Am I preparing myself through spiritual due diligence (prayer and the Word) so that the choice for integrity is already made when the test arrives?
- How can I speak truth to the authority I serve in a way that is respectful and honors their position?
- What commitment or decision do I need to refuse to preserve my moral freedom?

_____
_____
_____
_____
_____
_____
_____
_____
_____
_____
_____
_____
_____
_____
_____

The Steward's Seat

Anchor #10

Waiting,
Trusting,
Leading

The Steward's Seat

Anchor 10: Waiting, Trusting, Leading — The Endurance of Divine Timing

Leadership Reflection + Biblical Connection

Our professional culture has conditioned us to champion speed. We treat momentum as the ultimate strategy, where immediate action is often mistaken for true effectiveness. But the journey of stewardship teaches us that our timeline rarely aligns with the strategic plan we've laid out. The most profound development in a leader's life often happens not during the rush of execution, but during the period when the project feels temporarily stalled, the dots aren't connecting, we risk making the same mistake, the results are unclear, and our faith is truly tested.

Waiting is not emptiness. It is *formation.* It is a vital process where character is secured, roots are deepened, and we are prepared to handle the success we have been promised. Leaders who cannot wait often try to force outcomes, sacrificing long-term integrity for short-term results. The immediate driver to deliver, to prove relevance, and to keep the organization moving can drive us to act out of impatience rather than conviction.

Divine timing in leadership is, in truth, God's active orchestration of the environment. It may not feel great in the moment, but in the end, it's working out for the good; we just can't see it yet! We feel the pressure of the clock, and the natural response is to view any delay as an obstacle, yet this experience often reveals God's strategic design. Divine timing is not simply delayed timing, but rather it is strategic timing designed to ensure that when the breakthrough comes, the foundational readiness matches the size of the success.

The story of Abraham is the ultimate testament to this anchor. God promised him a son, a nation, and an enduring legacy when he was seventy-five years old. Then came the silence. Years passed. The promise remained, but the physical evidence deteriorated. Abraham and his wife Sarah grew very old. When the delay felt like a denial, they attempted to force the outcome through human intervention: Sarah offered her servant Hagar to Abraham to produce an heir. This was a decision driven by impatience and self-reliance, mistaking God's timing for God's inability. It took twenty-five years from the moment of the promise to the birth of the promised son, Isaac.

The lesson is that what God intends to give you cannot be produced by your own strength or by bending the rules of the process. The long delay was the laboratory for Abraham's steadfastness. The waiting prepared his heart and refined his reliance on God alone. The greatest fruit of waiting is not what you receive, but who you become. You learn to lead with a confidence rooted not in your ability *to force things forward*, but in your ability to *trust the unseen hand of your Father.* Delays are not denials. They are declarations that the result will be undeniably divine.

Leadership in Real Life

How the Call Takes Shape in Everyday Leadership

When you find yourself waiting in modern leadership, whether for a proposal to be approved, a promotion to land, a team to mature, or an organization to grow, your practice during that time becomes your highest act of leadership. Leadership in action often means respecting executive timelines, clarifying sudden changes with your team, resisting the urge to force outcomes, and using the pause to strengthen your internal systems.

Here, leadership demands the costly discipline to resist reaction. Rather than scramble, you invest in processes, relationships, and preparation so when opportunity arrives, you are ready.

The Reward and the Responsibility

Honoring divine timing strengthens inner confidence and earns the trust of others, showing that steady commitment matters more than approval. This steadfastness builds trust in the eyes of those around you, proving that your long-term commitment outweighs your need for short-term validation.

The responsibility is carrying the emotional fear that creeps in, the voice that says the moment has passed, or that you have been forgotten. You must actively anchor your worth in the promise and the goal, not the current timeline, especially when external results seem slow. And you must guard the morale of the people you lead, helping them see waiting as intentional formation and not accidental stagnation.

Leading Whole

Lead whole by intentionally declaring your dependence daily. Surrender your timeline to God in prayer every morning. Use the pause to invest in the internal development (reading, mentoring, journaling, etc.) that prepares you to successfully manage the inevitable increase when momentum finally breaks.

Your job during the wait is not to move the mountains. It is to prepare the soil. When you lead from a place of radical trust, you invite God's timing to override your ambition. Start trading the anxiety of human effort for the peace of dependability.

Prayer

Father,

I am often tempted to force outcomes, generate my own solutions and to believe that if I don't act now, there's no going back. Forgive me for confusing Your perfect timing with my urgent timeline.

Grant me the courage and the steadfastness of Abraham. Help me use this season of waiting as intentional formation, building character and capacity that will serve the long game. Teach me to pray without ceasing and to plan without panic.

I surrender my timeline, my ambition, and my need for immediate results. I choose to anchor my hope in Your promise and goal, not the shifting circumstances around me. Remind me that You are working, even when I cannot see it. Help me lead this season with trust.

In Jesus' name, Amen.

Leadership Check-In

- What project or decision am I currently trying to force that God may be asking me to surrender to divine timing?
- What is the biggest fear I am wrestling with during this period of waiting (e.g., being forgotten, failure, loss of influence)?
- How can I use this current pause to invest in internal formation (skill development, relationship building, personal spiritual practice)?
- What is one specific way I can communicate the value of waiting to the people I lead?
- Am I anchoring my sense of worth in the promise, or in the speed of the current process?

The Steward's Seat

Anchor #11

Finishing Well

The Steward's Seat

Anchor 11: Finishing Well — The Graceful Act of Release

Leadership Reflection + Biblical Connection

Leadership is not only measured by what we build but by how we release. It is easy to start strong, but the hardest work of stewardship is often the ending. At this moment, the final transition and the handing over of responsibility is the ultimate test of our professional integrity. The ability to surrender an assignment cleanly defines the true maturity of a leader.

The temptation to cling to a position, project, title, or anything is real. Years of dedication can make letting go feel impossible, tempting us to unintentionally micromanage successors or ensure we remain perpetually indispensable. The steward must realize that a clingy departure or handoff damages the assignment and hinders the future leader's ability to take ownership. Finishing well is the highest act of non-possessiveness.

The temptation to linger is often rooted in what I think is the myth of necessity. We convince ourselves that the assignment *needs* our continued insight when, in reality, our presence often crowds the necessary space for the next leader's authority to grow. True maturity means knowing when your contribution shifts from being essential to being an obstacle. The maturity of release requires celebrating the potential of the successor more than celebrating your own past success. It is also recognizing that your final act of devotion is ensuring the future is stronger than your past tenure.

The Bible offers vivid examples of leaders exiting at the right time, showing how God directs each transition for His purpose.

Elijah and Elisha: The Empowerment of Release

Elijah knew his season was ending, and he did not fight his departure or attempt to dilute his successor's authority. Instead, he invested fully in Elisha, allowing Elisha to witness the final miraculous works and commissioning him publicly. In a profound act of release, Elijah's mantle, the symbol of his authority, fell upon Elisha (2 Kings 2). This was not a passive handoff; it was deliberate and complete empowerment. Elijah secured his enduring impact not by staying, but by facilitating the next chapter. This transfer was complete, decisive, and empowering. He understood that his purpose was to serve his season, not to own the future.

Moses and Joshua: The Timing of Surrender

The passing of authority from Moses to Joshua is another powerful study in timing. Moses was explicitly instructed by God to commission Joshua publicly (Deuteronomy 31). This was not an exit due to failure, but a deliberate act of surrender to divine timing. Moses transferred authority while he was still strong, ensuring the people witnessed the full transfer of the mantle. This prevented ambiguity, honored God's timeline, and empowered Joshua's leadership from day one.

For the steward, the final act of leadership is not just leaving the room or assignment but ensuring the person who comes next is fully equipped, fully trusted, and fully empowered to succeed. This discipline secures the legacy of the entire purpose.

Leadership in Real Life

How the Call Takes Shape in Everyday Leadership

Finishing well is not an accident or something you stumble into. It is a meticulously executed exit strategy and it takes time. It looks like documenting institutional memory, streamlining processes, and ensuring your successor has the complete context necessary to manage the assignment. The highest form of wisdom in this stage is resisting the urge to offer uninvited advice once you have stepped back. The next leader must feel equipped, not managed from the sidelines.

The steward must be prepared for this final stage. When you leave a role, your importance and daily functional value changes overnight. You must manage the inevitable feeling of being unneeded. This is where the internal stature forged in the middle (Anchor 5) proves its worth. You must anchor your identity not in the assignment itself, but in the dependability of your character and how faithfully you carried out the assignment up until handoff.

The Reward and the Responsibility

The reward of a graceful release is watching the purpose continue and deepen, knowing you contributed to its sustainability. Your legacy is confirmed when the talent and organization flourish without you. Your final act proves that your identity was never tied to just the operational load, allowing you to walk away with peace. The deepest fulfillment is witnessing the assignment flourish in a new direction, which confirms that your entire tenure was dedicated to sustainability, not personal control. **Your legacy is secured when the purpose thrives without your daily oversight.**

The responsibility of this stage is the active work of empowerment. Your duty is to ensure the assignment's integrity is absolute, regardless of who or what takes over. You must commit to non-interference, ensuring the next leader has the space to lead differently, grow, and make their own mistakes.

Leading Whole

Lead whole by prioritizing closure and completeness. Pray for the continuity of the purpose. Release your old role to the organization fully, trusting God's selection and timing. Celebrate the future of the assignment and make space for new ideas and directions to take root. Practice the belief that true leadership is about increasing the success of others.

Finishing well requires the courage to say, "My work here is done, and I trust what comes next." As I once recently told a trusted executive mentor, *"The greatest gift I can give the person who comes after me is to hand them the baton much stronger than how I received it."* This is the ultimate, humble surrender of influence, and it is the sign of a steward who successfully navigated the entire journey. While the formal handover is complete, remember there is nothing wrong with offering yourself up to be a trusted sounding board, advisor, or mentor behind the scenes for the future leadership, if requested.

Prayer

Father,

Thank You for entrusting me with this assignment and for sustaining me throughout this season.

Grant me the courage and grace to finish this assignment well. Help me prepare the path for the next leader with wisdom, providing everything necessary for their success. Give me the humility of

Elijah and Moses, who knew when to step aside completely so that the next season could begin.

I ultimately release this role, its responsibilities, and its outcomes into Your sovereign hands. I choose to anchor my worth in the character You have built in me, not in the title I am leaving behind. May my departure bring stability, and my final act reflect Your faithfulness.

In Jesus' name, Amen.

Leadership Check-In

- What does a complete, non-possessive handover look like for the assignments I currently manage?
- Where do I feel the greatest toll of fearing irrelevance, and what spiritual truth do I need to anchor there?
- Am I actively documenting and empowering the next person or preparing a scenario where only I hold the key?
- If I were judged solely on how I exit, what discipline would I need to integrate immediately?

Anchor # 12

Legacy from
the Second
Chair

The Steward's Seat

Anchor 12: Legacy from the Second Chair — The Enduring Impact of Unseen Influence

Leadership Reflection + Biblical Connection

You have successfully navigated the entire journey of the Steward's Seat and understand the **gravity** of influence, the **courage** of integrity, and the **grace** of release. Now, the final question remains: what does legacy look like when you govern from the operational heart of an assignment?

The Second Chair is a *metaphor*, not necessarily a *position* or *title*. It is the strategic link, sitting at the intersection of vision and reality. This may very well be a second in command, but fundamentally, it is any position whose function is to integrate and execute the vision of the principal and to steward organizational completeness. This multi-dimensional role requires simultaneous translation: you must manage the aspirational language of the visionary while interpreting that into achievable practice for the people you lead. This crucial integration is what makes you a primary heartbeat of the organization.

For leaders who possess the gift of administration, legacy is measured by the enduring health and growth of the system you helped build and the people you helped elevate. Your legacy *is* the evidence that the organization can flourish not only after you leave, but because of how you governed the foundations while you were present.

The highest contribution of the leader in your role is to serve as the *chief stabilizer*. You are the one who ensures the rhythm is steady, the flow of resources is clear, and purpose is protected. This unique contribution is what makes your legacy powerful and lasting.

We must be honest about the weight of this role because it's not talked about or acknowledged much. You are the one responsible for seeing implications five moves ahead, while others are often simply focused on completing the task in front of them. Your job is to safeguard the foundation when others are tempted to trade discipline for speed. That means long nights running scenarios, anticipating political dynamics, and making decisions that affect the *whole*, not just the *moment*.

And yes, it gets exhausting, and it's totally okay to say that out loud! The fatigue comes from being the person who must insist on clarity, alignment, and structural integrity when it would be far easier to just "let things roll." Every organization, no matter how strong, naturally drifts towards informality, shortcuts, and speed from time to time – unless someone holds the line. That tension doesn't always feel good, but it is vital. You are the stabilizer. The standard-bearer. The one who keeps the house standing when others only see the room they're standing in.

I find deep fulfillment in better, more sustainable systems. But there is no greater joy than working for a CEO, Pastor, or Senior Executive who unequivocally trusts you; who feels, without question, that while things may not always be perfect, the **assignment is in good hands and will remain steady**. That level of unconditional confidence is a gift I have never taken lightly, nor should you. That's a part of your influence and legacy.

One of the Bible's best examples of administrative legacy comes through the Apostle Paul. While he was the visionary, he knew the enduring success of his apostleship depended on the carriers he established: Timothy and Titus. Paul didn't just teach them doctrine, but he also taught them how to build sustainable structures. His guidance to Titus, who was left to organize the churches in Crete, is a blueprint for administrative legacy. Furthermore, Paul's letters often required Timothy and Titus to correct deep spiritual and organizational misalignments. This indicates that the job of the carrier frequently involves the unpopular task of calling things out and enforcing the ethical baseline when the community is drifting.

Timothy and Titus left a legacy not of their own personal fame, but of structural soundness and integrity. Their legacy is the very existence and endurance of the early church itself. They built the systems and appointed the people who ensured the vision could survive the visionary. The ultimate result of their administrative leadership was the creation of a durable, replicable model that allowed the Christian faith to scale and endure for centuries. Consider this scale: the initial mandate was to bring order to scattered house churches across a few Roman provinces. This structural foundation—the appointment of qualified local leaders and the establishment of shared operational standards—enabled the faith to grow from a small, local movement of hundreds to a global religion of millions within three centuries. This model allowed the faith to expand beyond regional borders, establishing self-governing churches and a universal spiritual authority that survived political empires and cultural shifts.

For the leader in your position, this is the ultimate validation: you are the legacy architect. You helped build, through partnership and collaboration, the secure foundation that allowed others to reach the high places of the purpose.

Leadership in Real Life

How the Call Takes Shape in Everyday Leadership

Legacy from the Second Chair is built daily through intentional acts of governance.

- You prioritize process over personality: You make steady strides to ensure the system is sturdy enough to withstand the whims or failings of any individual.
- You build benches, not empires: You champion mentorship and empower multiple people so that knowledge is distributed and the organization does not buckle when there are exits. Longevity requires shared strength, not centralized power.
- You champion the unsung: You aim to direct acknowledgment toward those who are serving faithfully in the trenches, reinforcing the culture of stewardship that you embody.

The Reward and the Responsibility

The reward is profound: Legacy from the second chair is measured by continuity. You have built something that outlives your tenure. You helped cultivate an organizational culture that is stronger, steadier, and more aligned than how you found it. Fulfillment comes from knowing that your leadership protected purpose. The structures you helped build can withstand transition, personality shifts, and external pressure. This is legacy: the unseen work that allows the mission to continue with integrity over time.

The responsibility, however, is just as meaningful. To lead from the steward's seat is to recognize that your impact is not complete until it has been **passed on through *seed* planting**. Legacy requires transfer. It asks you to move beyond managing the work to developing the people who will one day inherit it. It means narrating your decisions, distilling your judgment, and teaching others how to see the system, not just the task. It also means cultivating leaders who can think across silos, honor process, and discern timing.

This is not about ensuring they replicate you.

It is about ensuring they can sustain the assignment.

Second chair leadership is never just operational — it is formational. I vividly remember a vulnerable time in my leadership journey when things were unusually tough. I began questioning if I was even the right fit for the organization, willing to walk away for what I thought was the greater good. However, my boss stopped me and said: *"What I need is for the system to align around you—you represent exactly what this place needs."* That moment taught me that as you serve, you aren't just filling a role; you are shaping thought patterns, strengthening decision-making muscles, and building a shared wisdom. Your true legacy is the internal coherence of the organization—the way it moves, thinks, and remains grounded long after your tenure ends.

So, the enduring responsibility is this: Leave strength behind. Leave clarity. Leave alignment. Leave a pathway that does not require your presence to remain intact. Legacy is not what you held together while you were there. Legacy is what *continues* to hold once you are gone.

Leading Whole

To lead whole means your legacy is shaped by ***who you are*** long before it is measured by ***what you built***. Administration is not all about control or being the one who "keeps everyone in line." It is a spiritual mandate to bring order, clarity, and steadiness. The work may be technical, but the source is deeply personal. **Your character**

is the operating system.

Leading whole requires a rhythm of renewal. Your clarity, your judgment, and your restraint are only as strong as your ability to stay grounded. Ethical consistency isn't just a virtue here; it's the backbone of your entire influence. When pressure rises, *your steadiness becomes the climate control for the organization.*

And in the end, your real legacy isn't the projects you touched or the initiatives you shepherded. It will be the cultural backbone that remains because you were there and the pieces you built around you. The professionalism you normalized. The patience and authenticity you modeled. When history is written, your chapter will show you helped shape the conditions that allowed the work to last.

Prayer

Father,

Thank You for entrusting me with the gift of administration and for placing me in this influential role. Grant me the courage to lead as a true legacy architect, building systems and developing people. Help me model structural soundness like Titus and Timothy, ensuring that my influence secures the organization's enduring health.

I choose to find my reward in knowing I honored You with my work. Let the legacy of my service be sustainability, not dependency.

In Jesus' name, Amen.

Leadership Check-In

- What is the single greatest structural weakness in the organization right now, and what action can I take this week to strengthen the foundation before I move on?
- Am I actively mentoring a potential successor to ensure overarching insight is successfully transferred?

- Looking backward: Does my character—the integrity I modeled day-to-day—align with the legacy I want to leave?
- If I were to step away tomorrow, what area would experience the most disruption, and what structure can I build now to strengthen it?
- Looking forward: How can I more intentionally give acknowledgment to another unsung leader and reinforce the culture of stewardship that you want to leave behind?

The Steward's Seat

The Steward's Seat

Bonus #13

The Steward's Daily Armor

The Steward's Seat

The Steward's Daily Armor: Why Daily Prep Matters

Every leader starts the day with a ritual, though those rituals look very different. Some start with coffee before the house wakes up. Others open their phone and dive straight into emails. Some review their calendar, already calculating the hours before the first meeting begins. These are the habits that help us get out the door, but preparation for a steward goes deeper than a checklist. We are not only called to manage tasks but entrusted with people, vision, and influence. And that means how we prepare each day determines how we lean into our calling.

I can remember seasons when I rushed from one responsibility to another, thinking that if my schedule was mapped out, I was ready. Then the day would hit. An unexpected conversation. A decision that juggled competing priorities. A colleague's discouragement landing squarely on my shoulders. My preparation had covered my tasks, but not my heart. My schedule accounted for time, but not my spirit.

That is when the words of Paul in Ephesians were reintroduced by my Pastor and began to completely reshape how I started each day. Everything we truly need for daily preparation is already written there: Put on the whole armor of God. He was not only speaking about spiritual battles. He was describing a way to step into each day with strength, clarity, and readiness.

For me, it starts at 5 a.m., in prayer, before phones buzz and the world demands my attention. In those quiet moments, I give thanks for new mercies and grace. I cover what I know is ahead, and I pray over the meetings and responsibilities I can see on my calendar. But here is the truth: one time is not always enough. By midday, distractions, interruptions, and competing demands can chip away at the peace and clarity I began with. And then comes the afternoon with a high-stakes meeting or a moment where others are looking to me for direction. That is when I have to pause and "armor up" again. Not because I failed earlier, but because stewardship requires strength that does not come from me alone.

This is why Paul calls it the whole armor of God. Every piece matters. If we leave one behind, we step into the day unprepared. But when we rise with the belt of truth, the breastplate of righteousness, the shoes of peace, the shield of faith, the helmet of salvation, and the sword of the Spirit, we are ready not only for what we expect, but also for what we cannot see.

The Steward's Daily Armor

Armor of God	Spiritually Prepares You	Leadership Application
Belt of Truth	Anchors you in God's Word and honesty, keeping you steady against lies and confusion.	Anchors your leadership in integrity. Truth-telling builds trust, and trust is the belt that holds everything else together.
Breastplate of Righteousness	Protects your heart from pride, envy, and wrong motives.	Guards your leadership decisions, ensuring you choose what is right over what is easy or popular.
Shoes of Peace	Positions you to walk in calm assurance, steady even when uncertainty surrounds you.	Sets the tone in every room you walk into. A steward's peace creates clarity and and opens space for solutions.
Shield of Faith	Deflects discouragement, doubt, and spiritual attack. Keeps you anchored in God's promises.	Deflects negativity, office politics, and cynicism. Faith keeps your eyes fixed on the mission, not the distractions.
Helmet of Salvation	Protects the mind with the assurance of who you are in Christ.	Secures your mindset. You walk into the day knowing who you are and why you are here, not shaken by critics or distractions.
Sword of the Spirit	Scripture and prayer cut through confusion and deception.	Your words carry weight. Speaking clarity, wisdom, and conviction cuts through noise, moves teams, and shapes culture.

Daily Practice: Putting On the Armor

Here is one way to make this more than words on a page:

- Begin your morning by reading **Ephesians 6:10–18** out loud.
- Pause and "put on" each piece of armor in prayer:
  - "Lord, today I fasten the belt of truth…"
  - "I cover my heart with the breastplate of righteousness…"
  - "I prepare my steps with shoes of peace…"
  - "I lift the shield of faith to guard against negativity and doubt…"
  - "I place on the helmet of salvation to protect my thoughts and perspective…"
  - "I take up the sword of the Spirit to lead and speak with wisdom today…"
- Identify one place in your leadership where you will need that specific armor.
  - Shoes of Peace? Maybe it's a challenging meeting.
  - Shield of Faith? Maybe it's a project where you feel stretched thin.
  - Sword of the Spirit? Maybe it's a presentation where your words will shape the path forward.
- Write one simple intention in your journal: "Today I will walk in peace as I lead the afternoon meeting."

Leadership Check-In

- Which piece of armor do I most often forget to put on?
- Where today did I notice myself leading without preparation?
- How did beginning my day with spiritual preparation change the way I approached leadership?
- What would it look like to "armor up" again before stepping into a new room or role today?

Closing Encouragement

Stewards do not simply prepare agendas or schedules. We prepare ourselves to carry responsibility with faithfulness and strength. Every day brings unknowns, but you do not have to walk into them uncovered. **Reality will hit, and there will be days when things don't go as planned, when you experience a sudden low, or when you face failure. But because you are armored, your foundation remains secure.** When you rise in the morning and put on the armor of God—and when you pause to put it on again as needed—you carry both spiritual and practical readiness. This is how you bridge faith and leadership. This is how you live and lead well.

The Steward's Seat

The Steward's Seat

159

About the Author
Ashely D. Teasdel

Ashely D. Teasdel is a thought leader and cultivator of purpose who thrives at the intersection of faith and practical leadership. With more than 15+ years of experience across government, ministry, banking, and business, she equips leaders to show up with clarity, conviction, and courage.

She currently serves in senior leadership for South Carolina's lead economic development cabinet agency, helping guide statewide strategy and growth. Her background also includes years serving as Chief of Staff at the Emmanuel Church of Our Lord Jesus Christ during a season of transformational growth.

Through her venture, Seeds of Leadership, Ashely walks alongside emerging and established leaders as a thought partner and encourager. She believes leadership is legacy—shaped, not by position, but by character, service, and alignment with God.

She resides in South Carolina with her husband and two daughters.

Speaking
Keynotes that inspire, encourage, challenge, and equip leaders with practical leadership and faith-forward insight.

Books & Leadership Resources
Devotionals, workbooks, and guides that strengthen purpose, clarity, and confidence, supporting leaders in both personal and professional growth.

The Leader's Corner Micro-Podcast
Short, impactful episodes on Spotify designed to spark reflection, offer practical leadership insight, and equip listeners with small moments of wisdom for their everyday work.

     www.sow2harvest.com

www.ingramcontent.com/pod-product-compliance
Lightning Source LLC
Chambersburg PA
CBHW070923130626
46555CB00001B/262